English Springer Spaniel

By Anne Hutchinson

BREEDERS' BEST™
A KENNEL CLUB BOOK®

ENGLISH SPRINGER SPANIEL

ISBN: 1-59378-933-5

Copyright © 2005

Kennel Club Books, LLC
308 Main Street, Allenhurst, NJ 07711 USA
Printed in South Korea

PHOTOS BY:
Paulette Braun,
Sherise Buhagiar, Ruth Dehmel,
Family Tree Portraits,
Isabelle Français, Alex Smith
and Karen Taylor

DRAWINGS BY:
Yolyanko el Habanero

Contents

CHAPTER 1

Meet the Springer Spaniel

If you are a fan of the spaniel breeds, you are bound to love the English Springer. This is a most jovial fellow who brims with zest and energy. He loves people and is always ready to play with family, friends, the plumber or whoever happens to visit! He's an excellent student: intelligent, eager to learn and anxious to please. His medium size makes him ideal for house or apartment life if given enough exercise.

The Springer is a handsome fellow who sports a dense double coat of

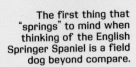

The first thing that "springs" to mind when thinking of the English Springer Spaniel is a field dog beyond compare.

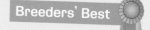
medium length. It can be flat or wavy, fringed with longer feathering in the appropriate places. The coat is most attractive, but it does require regular grooming to keep it looking tidy and free of mats and tangles. The show-bred Springer generally carries a longer, heavier coat than does the field-bred type. All Springers, however, shed somewhat year-round, and while routine grooming will help to minimize the amount of dead hair, prospective owners should be prepared to live with dog hair throughout the house.

The field-type Springer is typically a finer-boned dog with less feathering on the coat.

Both show- and field-bred Springers are loving and devoted dogs, easy to train and delightful to live with. Their temperaments can range from laid-back and easygoing to highly energetic. The Springer's pedigree and purpose (field or show) are major factors in determining his person-

The show-type Springer has heavier bone and a more abundant coat with long feathering.

ality; the field Springer is more spirited and vivacious, but both types share the same love of family and friends.

Of the eight spaniel breeds recognized by the American Kennel Club, the Springer reigns as the flushing specialist most popular with the American sportsman. This comes as no surprise, as the Springer's hunting and flushing ability has been recounted for centuries in literature and artwork. Historical records refer to dogs called spaniels as early as 450 AD. It is believed that this and other spaniel types originated in Spain, with the

The Springer is an all-weather dog who is not afraid to get wet. His double coat is ideally suited for land and water work, making this talented hunting companion a favorite in the field.

name "spaniel" arising from *Hispania*, which is the Latin word for Spain.

Reference to "spanyells" occurs in writings dating back to 1392. These spaniel dogs were used to "spring" or flush game for the hunters, startling their prey for the nets, hawks and hounds that were used during that era to snare the game. The specific designation of "Springer" began to appear in English literature during the 16th and 17th centuries. The increased use of firearms during that period created a demand for a dual-purpose dog in the field, one who would also retrieve the birds after they were flushed, and the Springer was the perfect candidate for such work.

During the early 1800s, Sir Thomas Boughey developed a specific line of Springers in his famous Aqualate Kennels. Although the breed remained as yet unnamed, Boughey kept a detailed stud book to keep records of his breeding program. About this same time, Springers from yet another prominent kennel became known as the "Norfolk Spaniel."

The Sporting Spaniel Society of Britain was founded in 1885. The club objected to the designation "Norfolk" and arranged to have the name changed back to Springer, at the same time drawing up a formal standard for the breed. In 1902, the British Kennel Club recognized the English Springer Spaniel as a distinct breed and awarded Springers their own classification.

With the official recognition of the Springer, breed championships naturally followed. Beechgrove Will, whelped in the late 1890s and owned by Winton Smith, became the first Springer to earn that distinction and did so in grand style by winning Challenge Certificates (awards that count toward a British championship) at the famed Crystal Palace Dog Show in London in 1902 and 1903, and then earning his champion title in 1906. Bench (show) champions of that period more closely resembled the

A working Springer and an American and Canadian Champion: This is "Spice," bred and co-owned by the author.

original Springer type, and most were dual-purpose dogs who hunted during their show career.

Early proponents of the breed emphasized that the Springer was essentially a working dog. Well-known breeders who produced champions in both venues included C.C. Eversfield and his Denne Springers, J.P. Gardener of Hagley Springers and Colonel Williams of Gerwyn Kennels in Wales. Chrishall Springers, owned by John and Godfrey Kent, produced the great English Field Champion Silverstar of Chrishall, who can be found in the pedigrees of many early American imports. The complete list of early dogs and owners who were important in the development of the English Springer Spaniel is far too numerous to duplicate here but can be found in historical tomes devoted to the breed.

The first documented Springer to be imported into North America was one that entered Canada in 1913. From that point on, the breed quickly gained popularity in both Canada and the United States. Many early exhibitors also competed in field trials, and it was not uncommon for fanciers to hunt their dogs one day and show them on the bench the next.

The English Springer Spaniel Field Trial Association (ESSFTA) was formed in 1924 and in 1926 became the American Kennel Club (AKC)-recognized parent club of the breed. The club's original aim was to promote the Springer both in the field and on the bench, something that it continues to do today. The first breed standard was drafted by the ESSFTA and approved by the AKC in 1927. Several revisions have followed with the latest approved in 1994.

From around the 1940s on, breeder specialization in either show or field pursuits has split today's Springer in the United States into what seems like two separate breeds, each bred to serve the breeder's particular purpose. In the United Kingdom, the breed's homeland, such a split has not occurred, and a North American English Springer show dog looks somewhat different from his British counterpart. In the US, the field-bred Springer is the ultimate athlete, capable of sterling performance in the field, but is smaller and finer-boned than his show dog counterpart. The conformation-show prospect may better exemplify breed type, but may or may not hunt successfully or with the speed and style of the field-bred dog. A few show lines have retained their field instincts, but even those do not have the verve and vigor of the field-bred Springer.

As a result, today's English Springer Spaniel is basically two distinct varieties within the same breed. One is a handsome fellow who is soft-wired and can be shown in the conformation ring, and the other is a high-flying field-trial contender who will hunt enthusiastically and compete in field events. A few lines of Springers lie somewhere in between. Be forewarned, however—any of the types will steal your heart, and make a fine family pet.

MEET THE SPRINGER SPANIEL

Overview

- The Springer is a popular, friendly, outgoing dog known traditionally for his skills in the field but also for his appeal as a show dog, thus the emergence of two distinct Springer types.
- The Springer, and spaniels in general, may have Spanish roots, but the breed first gained a foothold in England.
- Although the breed existed long before this, the name English Springer Spaniel did not become official until the early 20th century.
- The breed's first appearance in North America was in the early 20th century in Canada, entering the US soon after. Today the Springer is an all-around favorite in both countries.

Description of the Springer

If any breed standard were designed to preserve the true type and purpose of a breed, it is that of the English Springer Spaniel. The Springer is first and foremost a "sporting dog of distinct spaniel character" that is both beautiful and utilitarian. The standard, written by the parent club and accepted by the AKC, sets forth detailed guidelines intended to promote the breed's uniform characteristics while still preserving its original purpose: to hunt and find game.

That said, we've discussed how

Initially, the most noticeable difference in the show type is his abundance of coat, although there are other differences as well.

today's Springer has been split into two types, one for the field and the other for conformation. Each is distinctly different from the other in aspects such as size, head type, ears, coat type, markings and hunting ability. Show Springers have been bred primarily according to the written standard for the breed and thus display more uniformity in structure and appearance. They are more heavily boned and evenly proportioned, with well-chiseled heads and flat coats that sport long, luxurious feathering. Coat colors are typically black or liver with white markings or tricolor; black and white or liver and white with tan markings, usually found on eyebrows, cheeks, inside of the ears and under the tail.

A show Springer in full coat presents a striking silhouette.

The field Springer is a true athlete, more agile than the show type, bred for the hunter's pleasure and the beauty of the work at hand. This type also is usually smaller, with

The eyes are a key feature of the breed's appeal and looking at this soulful Springer, there's no wonder why!

finer bone. His coat is generally shorter, coarse and somewhat curly. His markings may be any combination of the standard colors, with white frequently the dominant color, which gives the hunter better visibility in the field. Head type can vary from square to narrow, muzzles may be wide or snipy and ears are often shorter with less feathering. Hunting prowess is of primary concern; in the field-bred Springer, form always follows function.

The following description of the English Springer Spaniel is excerpted from the AKC's breed standard. For the full standard, which includes faults and disqualifications, visit www.akc.org.

General Appearance: The English Springer Spaniel is a medium-sized sporting dog, with a compact body and a docked tail. His coat is moderately long, with feathering on his legs, ears, chest and brisket. His pendulous ears, soft gentle expression, sturdy build and friendly wagging tail proclaim him unmistakably a member of the ancient family of spaniels. He is above all a well-proportioned dog, free from exaggeration, nicely balanced in every part. He looks the part of a dog that can go, and keep going, under difficult hunting conditions...and is every inch a sporting dog of distinct spaniel character.

Size, Proportion, Substance: He is to be kept to medium size. Ideal height at the shoulder for dogs is 20 inches; for bitches, it is 19 inches. A 20 inch dog, well-proportioned and in good condition, will weigh approximately 50 pounds; a 19 inch bitch will weigh approximately 40 pounds. The length of the body (measured from point of shoulder to point of buttocks) is slightly greater than the height at the withers.

Head: The head is impressive without being

heavy. Its beauty lies in a combination of strength and refinement. It is important that its size and proportion be in balance with the rest of the dog. The eyes, more than any other feature, are the essence of the Springer's appeal. Ears are long and fairly wide, hanging close to the cheeks with no tendency to stand up or out. Correct ear set is on a level with the eye and not too far back on the skull. The skull is medium-length and fairly broad, flat on top and slightly rounded at the sides and back. The nostrils are well-opened and broad. Teeth are strong, clean, of good size and ideally meet in a close scissors bite.

Neck, Topline, Body: The neck is moderately long, muscular, clean and slightly arched at the crest. It blends gradually and smoothly into sloping shoulders. The portion of the topline from withers to tail is firm and slopes very gently. The body

is short-coupled, strong and compact. The chest is deep, reaching the level of the elbows, with well-developed forechest. The back is straight, strong and essentially level. The tail is carried

Two field dogs, right at home in the tall grass, ready for action.

horizontally or slightly elevated and displays a characteristic lively, merry action, particularly when the dog is on game.

Forequarters: Efficient movement in front calls for proper forequarter assembly. The shoulder blades are flat and fairly close together at

English Springer Spaniel

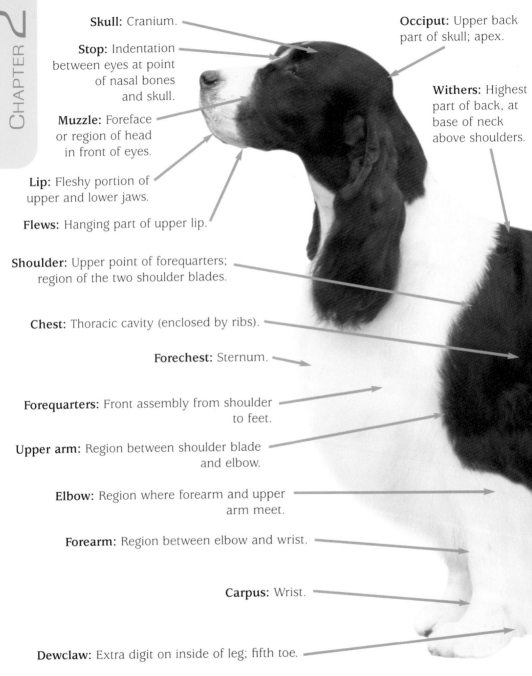

Skull: Cranium.

Stop: Indentation between eyes at point of nasal bones and skull.

Muzzle: Foreface or region of head in front of eyes.

Lip: Fleshy portion of upper and lower jaws.

Flews: Hanging part of upper lip.

Shoulder: Upper point of forequarters; region of the two shoulder blades.

Chest: Thoracic cavity (enclosed by ribs).

Forechest: Sternum.

Forequarters: Front assembly from shoulder to feet.

Upper arm: Region between shoulder blade and elbow.

Elbow: Region where forearm and upper arm meet.

Forearm: Region between elbow and wrist.

Carpus: Wrist.

Dewclaw: Extra digit on inside of leg; fifth toe.

Occiput: Upper back part of skull; apex.

Withers: Highest part of back, at base of neck above shoulders.

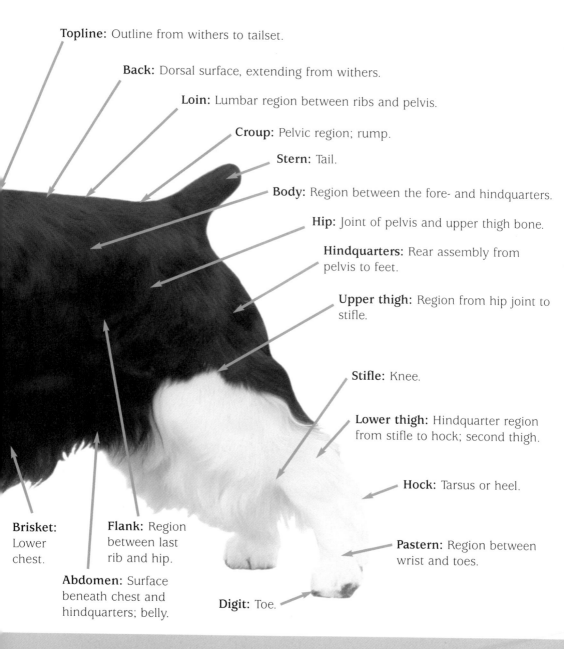

Topline: Outline from withers to tailset.

Back: Dorsal surface, extending from withers.

Loin: Lumbar region between ribs and pelvis.

Croup: Pelvic region; rump.

Stern: Tail.

Body: Region between the fore- and hindquarters.

Hip: Joint of pelvis and upper thigh bone.

Hindquarters: Rear assembly from pelvis to feet.

Upper thigh: Region from hip joint to stifle.

Stifle: Knee.

Lower thigh: Hindquarter region from stifle to hock; second thigh.

Hock: Tarsus or heel.

Pastern: Region between wrist and toes.

Brisket: Lower chest.

Flank: Region between last rib and hip.

Abdomen: Surface beneath chest and hindquarters; belly.

Digit: Toe.

CHAPTER 2

the tips, molding smoothly into the contour of the body. The shoulder blade and upper arm are of apparent equal length, forming an angle of nearly 90 degrees. Elbows lie close to the body. Forelegs are straight with the same degree of size continuing to the foot. Pasterns are short, strong and slightly sloping. Feet are round or slightly oval. They are compact and well-arched, of medium size with thick pads.

The English Springer is a medium-sized dog with a compact body and a friendly nature. The essence of the Springer shows on this dog's smiling face.

Hindquarters: The Springer should be worked and shown in hard, muscular condition with well-developed hips and thighs. His whole rear assembly suggests strength and driving power. The feet are the same as in front, except that they are smaller and often more compact.

Coat: The Springer has an outer coat and an undercoat. On the body, the outer coat is of medium length, flat or wavy, and is easily distinguishable from the undercoat, which is short, soft and dense. The quantity of undercoat is affected by climate and season. When in combination, outer coat and undercoat serve to make the dog substantially waterproof, weatherproof and thorn-proof. On ears, chest, legs and belly, the Springer is nicely furnished with a fringe of feathering of moderate length and heaviness. On the head, front of the forelegs, and below the hock joints on the front of the hind legs, the hair is short and fine.

Color: All the following combinations of colors and

markings are equally acceptable:

(1) Black or liver with white markings or predominantly white with black or liver markings; (2) Blue or liver roan; (3) Tricolor: black and white or liver and white with tan markings, usually found on eyebrows, cheeks, inside of ears and under the tail. Any white portion of the coat may be flecked with ticking.

Gait: Balance is a prerequisite to good movement. The front and rear assemblies must be equivalent in angulation and muscular development for the gait to be smooth and effortless.

Temperament: The typical Springer is friendly, eager to please, quick to learn and willing to obey. Such traits are conducive to tractability, which is essential for appropriate handler control in the field. In the show ring, he should exhibit poise and attentiveness and permit himself to be examined by the judge without resentment or cringing.

DESCRIPTION OF THE SPRINGER

Overview

- Despite the split into show and field types, the breed standard aims to preserve the breed's original function and instincts.
- Abundance of coat, head shape and markings are among the differences in the two types; basically, show breeders concentrate primarily on form while field breeders concentrate primarily on function.
- The Springer is medium-sized and should not look exaggerated in any way. He should look like a sporting dog.
- A good Springer, no matter the type, possesses good overall appearance, sound movement and of course the breed's outgoing temperament.

CHAPTER 3

Are You a Springer Person?

The decision to buy a puppy is a momentous one for your entire family. It's also a very weighty decision that can spell disaster if you fail to choose the right breed of dog. If you're thinking spaniel thoughts and are considering the English Springer, be sure that you understand the characteristics of the breed before you bring one home.

Springers are true people-lovers who consider family, friends and

Are you ready for a dog who loves you and wants you to know it?

strangers as potential playmates. Just nod your head and he'll be ready for a game, a training session, a walk outdoors, just about whatever you're up for! If you're looking for a guard dog, however, this happy, friendly fellow does not fit that description.

A good owner for the Springer is someone who appreciates an athletic, versatile dog that enjoys all kinds of outdoor activities.

Springers are natural athletes and, as such, they require a great deal of daily exercise and activity. Yet despite their love of high-energy outdoor fun and games, they live best indoors with their people and will languish if they are isolated from the humans that they love.

Do they chew? Sure, all puppies chew. While not voracious chewers like Golden or Labrador Retrievers, Springers are still sporting dogs who love to retrieve game. All dogs that are bred to carry things in their mouths will have a tendency throughout their lives to chew whatever they can get their mouths on, so your shoes, socks and table

"Spirit," a 12-week-old puppy bred and co-owned by the author, shows the breed's natural instinct to retrieve birds.

legs are all potential "victims." A wise owner can minimize the damage and encourage appropriate chewing behavior by providing appropriate chew toys and teaching the Springer from the outset what he may and may not chew. Puppy owners who fail to dog-proof their homes or supervise their puppies tell horror stories about the impossible things that their Springers have chewed or consumed. If you are not willing to train your pup or supervise him, be prepared to face the consequences. Damage to your home or belongings will be the least of your worries if your dog injures himself or swallows something toxic.

Pucker up! There's no doubt that the Springer is a people-loving breed.

If you're a water lover, you will likely have an eager swimming companion in your Springer.

Springers are great with children and quickly will become best friends with your kids and their friends. They are medium-sized dogs and not difficult to handle, but they are still exuberant as puppies (and adults!), so both the dog and the children should be supervised whenever they are spending time together to prevent mishaps due to normal Springer enthusiasm. Most

Springers are also canine-friendly and get along well with other dogs and most four-legged family pets.

Are you prepared for dog hair? Springers have dense double coats that drop a little hair all year long. If dog hair on your furniture will drive you nuts, consider a breed with a different kind of coat.

What are your goals for your Springer pup? Today's Springers come in two

CHAPTER 3

different "packages," one bred for the show ring and the other bred for the breed's original purpose: to find, flush and retrieve game. As a hunting companion, the Springer is by far the most popular of the spaniel breeds. Just say "flushing spaniel" to a hunter

If you want to try your hand at showing, you must find a breeder who raises show-type Springers. The Springer is a good choice for a novice handler, as this is a friendly and biddable breed that will learn the rules of the ring quickly.

and he'll know that you are referring to the Springer. Then he will happily regale you with stories of his Springer's diving

into a thicket after a pheasant or leaping high into the air after the flushed bird...Springer poetry in its purest form.

For the conformation aficionado, the opposite is true. This fancier's vision is the perfectly proportioned Springer with pleasing markings, superb gait and a precise show stance that will capture the eye and heart of the conformation judge. For this person, the dog's field ability is less important or perhaps not important at all.

Whatever your goals, the Springer is an easy dog to train. He is bright and eager to please, but he also is a softie and will easily wilt if his owner is heavy-handed or too demanding. He will respond best to a training regimen filled with praise, praise and more praise.

Whether your passion lies in the field or in the show ring, or you are attracted to the breed solely for its virtues as a companion, adding a Springer to your family will dramatically alter your lifestyle. This dog needs exercise and plenty of it to stay physically and mentally fit; he also needs to be a true part of the family. Owning an English Springer Spaniel means committing to at least two brisk walks and adequate playtime every day, as well as sharing your family room, your activities and your life with a dog. Meeting those demands will enhance not only your Springer's life but yours as well.

It will be hard to resist the pleading eyes of a Springer pup...he can really turn on the charm!

ARE YOU A SPRINGER PERSON?

Overview

- Consider all of the breed's traits before deciding that the Springer is for you. This is an active, athletic, people-loving breed who makes a good home companion if given the proper amount of exercise.
- The Springer can be a very oral breed, remembering his instincts to carry shot birds to the hunter, so proper chewing habits must be instilled from puppyhood.
- Be prepared to devote some time to grooming and know that the Springer will shed at least lightly all year round.
- The Springer can be trained for a range of activities and loves to do things with his owners; he is good with children and generally has a lot to offer his family.

CHAPTER 4

Selecting a Breeder

Whether you plan to hunt with your Springer, show him in conformation or just enjoy him as a family companion, you want a healthy Springer pup with a good temperament and correct Springer structure and characteristics.

This little fellow should be with you for the next 12 or 13 years, so health and stability are primary concerns.

Your best source for a sound puppy is a reputable breeder, one

A good breeder will invite you and your family into his home to meet and get to know the puppies.

who has experience with the breed and who cares about the quality of the puppies he produces rather than the amount of money he might make selling his pups. It may take a bit more time to locate a good breeder, but do make that extra effort. You'll be glad you did.

Breeders should provide early socialization experiences for their pups. This litter enjoys the fresh air from the safety of a wire exercise pen.

A breeder/puppy search can be an emotionally trying experience, taxing your patience and your willpower. All puppies are adorable, and it's easy to fall in love with the first cute pup you see, but a poor-quality Springer will have health and temperament problems that can empty your wallet and, worse, break your heart. So do your breeder homework before you visit those cute pups. Arm yourself with a list of questions for the breeder, but leave your wallet and your kids at home so you aren't tempted to take home a poorly bred but nonetheless irresistible Springer pup.

Don't base your choice on looks alone! Ask the breeder to tell you all about the litter's background and his reasons behind the breeding.

So how do you find a reputable breeder whom you can trust? Dedicated breeders often belong to the breed's parent club and/or a local breed or kennel club. Such affiliation with other experienced breeders and sportsmen expands their knowledge of their chosen breed, which further enhances their credibility. Breed clubs require their member breeders to adhere to specific ethics in their breeding programs. Responsible breeders, by the way, do not raise several different breeds of dogs or produce multiple litters of pups throughout the year; one or two litters a year is typical. The parent club for the Springer, the English Springer Spaniel Field Trial Association (ESSFTA), can be found online at www.essfta.org, where you can find breed information

The breeder's advice and guidance will help you find the pup for you. You should have a good rapport with your breeder; she should be honest, accessible and eager to share her knowledge about the breed.

and make inquiries to be referred to breeders in your area.

Experienced Springer breeders are frequently involved in some aspect of the dog fancy with their dog(s), perhaps showing in conformation, hunt tests or field trials, or training them for other performance events or dog-related activities. Their Springer(s) may have earned titles in various areas of competition, which is added proof of the breeder's experience and commitment to the breed. Spend the day at a dog show or other dog event where you can meet breeders and exhibitors and get to know their dogs. Most Springer devotees are more than happy to show off their dogs and brag about their accomplishments. Any information gleaned from these conversations will make you a smarter shopper when you visit a litter of pups. Also, if you know a Springer of

whom you are fond, ask the owner where he got his dog; if he gives you a breeder's name, research that breeder.

As important as where to look is where *not* to look for your Springer puppy. Skip the puppy ads in your local newspaper. Reputable breeders rarely advertise in newspapers. They are very particular about prospective puppy owners and do not rely on mass advertising to attract the right people; rather, they depend on referrals from other breeders and previous puppy clients. Good breeders are more than willing to keep any puppy past the usual eight-week placement age until the right person comes along.

If you go to visit a breeder and you have any doubts at all, feel free to ask for references and check them out. It's unlikely that a breeder will volunteer the names of unhappy puppy clients, but calling other owners of the breeder's pups may make you more comfortable in dealing with that breeder.

When you have found a reputable breeder or two and you are ready to make some visits, know what to ask the breeder and what the breeder will want to know from you. For starters, always ask to see the litter's pedigrees and registration papers. Although AKC registration is no guarantee of quality, it is one small step in the right direction; further, if you hope to show your pup or enter AKC-licensed competitions, registration with the AKC is necessary.

The pedigree should include three to five generations of ancestry. Inquire about any titles in the pedigree. Titles simply indicate a dog's accomplishments in some area of canine competition, which proves the merits of the ancestors and adds to the breeder's credibility. While it is true that, like

the registration, a pedigree cannot guarantee health or good temperament, a well-constructed pedigree is still a good insurance policy and a good starting point. There should be no extra fee, by the way, for either the pedigree or registration papers. The AKC states that papers do not cost extra, and any breeder who charges for those documents is unscrupulous.

Ask the breeder why he planned this litter. A conscientious breeder plans a litter of Springers for specific reasons. He should explain the genetics behind this particular breeding and what he expects the breeding to produce. He never breeds a litter because "his Springer is charming and beautiful, his friend's dog is a handsome fellow, they will have adorable puppies," or so his children can experience the miracle of puppy birth. Furthermore, just loving his dog like crazy does not qualify any individual to breed dogs intelligently or to properly raise a litter of Springer pups.

Ask the breeder about health issues and clearances. Springers are prone to canine hip dysplasia (HD), a potentially crippling joint disease. Ask if the sire and dam have hip clearances from the OFA (Orthopedic Foundation for Animals, a national canine health registry), which they should in order to be considered for breeding. Have the parents' eyes been examined for progressive retinal atrophy (PRA, an inherited retinal disorder that can result in total blindness), and retinal dysplasia (a malformation of the retina) within the past year? Only a board-certified veterinary ophthalmologist is qualified and equipped to examine a dog's eyes for these heritable disorders. Eye clearances from the Canine Eye Registration Foundation (CERF) should be obtained on all breeding animals. Good breeders will

gladly, in fact proudly, provide these and other necessary health documents. Most health clearances (not just hips) on dogs in your pup's pedigree may be verified with a search of OFA records at www.offa.org.

The breeder's love of the Springer and of her dogs should be undeniable!

Other eye problems recognized in the Springer include entropion, a condition in which the eyelids are turned inward, toward the surface of the eye. In severe cases, the cornea can become bruised and inflamed, causing pain and eventual blindness. It can be corrected surgically, but entropion can be hereditary, so breeding from affected dogs should be avoided.

Seizure disorders, while not common, do occur in certain lines of Springers. Ask the breeder about the frequency of seizures within this pedigree and what measures they have taken to breed dogs as free of seizures as possible. Allergies and skin disorders occur in all breeds of dog. Some are seasonal, others persist year-round. Ask the breeder if the sire, dam or grandparents have experienced allergic symptoms.

Phosphofructokinase (PFK) deficiency is known to affect some lines of Springers. PFK is an enzyme vital to the tissues' ability to convert sugar into energy. Some dogs with PFK deficiency never display clinical signs, while those severely affected will suffer bouts of severe illness. PFK deficiency is detected through a blood test. Once

again, discuss this disorder with the breeder.

Temperament is of primary importance in the Springer. While proper Springer temperament is a joy to live with, a few Springers sadly have displayed what is known as "dominance aggression" (often inaccurately called "rage syndrome"). The affected dog will exhibit a normal temperament most of the time but occasionally go into a frenzy of rage in which he attacks anything that moves, whether human or otherwise. When the episode is over, the dog appears to have no recollection of what has happened. Although such instances are not common, the condition is a reality and cannot be dismissed when looking for a sound Springer puppy. Ask the breeder if he is familiar with this problem and if it exists at all in the puppy's pedigree.

You can research these and other Springer health

problems on the ESSFTA's website (www.essfta.org), which offers helpful and detailed articles on the diseases and problems seen in the breed.

When visiting the breeder, be prepared to answer

living arrangements (i.e., family, house, yard, kids, other pets, work schedule, etc.), your goals for the pup and how you plan to raise him. The breeder's primary concern is the future of his puppies and whether or not

The pups' living quarters should be clean and comfortable, in an area where they are exposed to the goings-on of the household.

questions, as a good breeder will ask you questions, too, about your dog history, previous dogs you have owned, breeds that you have experience with, if your dogs lived long lives with you, etc. He will want to know your

you and your family are suitable owners who will provide a proper and loving home for one of his precious little ones. You should be suspicious of any breeder who agrees to sell you a Springer puppy without any type of interrogation process. Such indifference indicates a lack of concern about the pups and casts doubt on the breeder's ethics and breeding program; this is a breeder of whom you should steer clear.

A good breeder also will warn you about the downside of the English Springer Spaniel. No breed of dog is perfect, nor is every breed suitable for every person's temperament and lifestyle. Be prepared to weigh the pros and cons of Springer ownership and be ready for the breeder to honestly assess you as a potential Springer owner.

If you proceed with the puppy process, there are a few more things you should know. In addition to giving you the pedigree and registration, most reputable breeders have a puppy sales contract that includes specific health guarantees and reasonable return policies. They should agree to accept a puppy back if things do not work out. They also should be willing, indeed anxious, to check up on the puppy's progress after he leaves home and be available if you have questions or problems with the pup. A good breeder will be a source of support for the dog's entire life.

You can expect to pay a dear price for all of these breeder qualities, whether you purchase a "pet-quality" Springer for a companion dog or one for show or hunting potential. The "discount" or "bargain" Springer, however, is not a bargain at all. Indeed, the discount pup in reality has little chance of developing into a healthy, stable adult. Such "bargains" could ultimately cost you a fortune in vet expenses as well as heartache that can't be measured in dollars and cents.

On the other hand, a pet-quality Springer from a good breeder should be as healthy, sound and personable as his show-potential littermates. Many breeders place their pet-quality puppies on limited registration with the AKC. This does register the pup with the AKC and allows the dog to compete in AKC-licensed competition, but does not allow AKC registration of any offspring from the mature dog. The purpose of a limited registration is to prevent indiscriminate breeding of "pet-quality" Springers. The breeder, and only the breeder, can cancel the limited registration if the adult dog develops into a breeding-quality animal.

Along with doing your research and knowing what to look for, an essential ingredient in your breeder search is patience. You will not likely find the right breeder or litter on your first go-round. Good breeders often have waiting lists, but a good Springer pup is worth the wait.

SELECTING A BREEDER

Overview

- A reputable breeder is the only source from which you should consider buying a puppy.
- Locate breeders through referrals from breed clubs, by talking with others in the breed and by visiting dog shows.
- Go through the pup's pedigree with the breeder. Also discuss hereditary health problems in the Springer and ask to see health-testing documentation proving the parents' good health.
- Be prepared to answer many questions from the breeder as he interviews you to ensure that you will provide a good home for one of his pups.
- A good breeder will be a source of support for you throughout your Springer's life.

Finding the Right Puppy

A lthough the English Springer Spaniel has earned a place of merit in the world of the hunter and the field trialer, it has not reached the popularity of the retrieving breeds. Finding a quality puppy may take a bit of research. Be prepared to travel to investigate a litter; if possible, visit more than one. You will be surprised at the difference from one litter to the next. Follow up on any referrals and take your time. After all, this pup will be with you for the next 12 or 13 years!

Springer puppies are enormously appealing, and you can

Watch the pups interact with their dam and with each other to see their individual personalities.

easily fall in love with the first cute puppy you see. However, you are choosing a future family member, and there are many traits to consider other than "adorable"... besides, all puppies are adorable! You need to evaluate the sire and dam, the breeder and the living environment in which the pups are being raised. You'll be a smarter shopper for your efforts and thus end up with a better pup.

These youngsters are not yet ready to leave for their new homes, but breeders often allow prospective owners to visit the litter and choose their pups a few weeks in advance.

Where and how a litter of pups is raised are vitally important to their early development into confident and social pups. The litter should be kept indoors, in the house, not isolated in a basement, garage or outside kennel building. A few very experienced breeders sometimes have separate kennel facilities for their adult dogs. However, all litters should be born and raised in the house until at least seven weeks of age.

When you meet the litter, you'll just want to scoop up an armful of Springer puppy love!

All Springer puppies need to be socialized daily with people and people activities. The greater the pups' exposure to household sights and sounds from birth, the easier their adjustment to their future human family.

During your visit, scrutinize the puppies as well as their living area for cleanliness and signs of sickness or poor health. The pups should be reasonably clean (allowing for normal non-stop "puppy-pies"). They should appear energetic, bright-eyed and alert. Healthy pups have clean, shiny coats, are well proportioned and feel solid and muscular without being overly fat and pot-bellied. Watch for crusted eyes or noses and any watery discharge from the nose, eyes or ears. Gums should be pink, not pale. Listen for coughing or mucousy sniffing or snorting. Check for evidence of watery or bloody stools. If you're looking for a show dog, the pigment of the nose and eyerims should match the color of the dog, either liver or black.

Visit with the dam and the sire, if possible. In many cases, the sire is not on the breeder's premises, but the breeder should have photos, his pedigree and a resume of his health certifications, his characteristics and accomplishments. Discuss the pedigrees and health backgrounds of both the dam and the sire. Just a note: the dam should be with the pups; if she is not, this is a red flag to move on and continue your puppy search with another breeder.

It is normal for some dams to be somewhat protective of their young, but overly aggressive or overly shy behavior is unacceptable. Springers are among the friendliest of creatures, and it's a rare Springer that will shrink from a friendly overture. Temperament is inherited, and if one or both parents are aggressive or excessively shy, it is likely that some of the pups will inherit those characteristics.

It's also normal for a new mother to have a rather scrawny coat or be on the thin side after weeks of nursing hungry pups. However, there is a big difference between normal post-partum appearance and signs of poor health or neglect.

Notice how the pups interact with their littermates and their surroundings, especially their responses to people. They should be active and outgoing. In most Springer litters, some pups will be more outgoing than others, but even a quiet pup that has been properly socialized should accept cuddling and gentle handling.

Temperament and behavior problems occur in all breeds of dog. Environmental factors as well as health and genetics influence adult canine behavior. It's important to select a stable puppy that is curious, outgoing and playful. He should not be timid or aggressive, nor should he resist being held and cuddled.

The breeder should be honest in discussing any

When you find the perfect puppy match, you will know it!

differences in puppy personalities and be willing to answer your questions about potential temperament problems. Although many breeders do some sort of temperament testing, they also have been with their pups since the litter's birth, cuddling and cleaning up after them, and by now know the subtle differences in each pup's personality. The breeder's observations and recommendations are valuable aids in selecting a Springer puppy that best suits your needs and lifestyle.

Some pups will show more promise than others for certain pursuits, and the breeder can help you select one with the most potential for meeting your long-term goals. If you're hoping for a hunting dog and the breeder has a supply of birds to test the pups, look for a puppy who gets excited at the sight or scent of feathers.

Do you prefer a male or a female? Both sexes are loving and loyal, and the differences are due more to individual personalities rather than to sex. The adult Springer female is a lovable girl and easy to live with but,

like females of most breeds, she can be affected by hormonal peaks if not spayed. The adult male is a bit taller and heavier than the female. He also will carry more coat. In male puppies, both testicles should be descended into the scrotum. A dog with undescended testicles will make a fine pet but will be ineligible to compete in the show ring.

Males of most breeds tend to be more physical and exuberant during adolescence, which can be problematic in an energetic sporting dog. An untrained male also can become dominant with people and other dogs, so he must respect you as his leader. Intact males also may be more territorial, especially with other male dogs. Altering your male or female Springer creates a level playing field and eliminates or at least diminishes most sex-related behaviors.

By eight weeks of age, the pups should have had at least one worming and first puppy shots, and should have certificates from the vet to verify their good health at the time of the exam. Prior to bringing home your puppy your breeder should give you a list of supplies you need to purchase to properly raise your Springer. The brand of food and amount to feed should be discussed with your breeder.

Good breeders also give their clients puppy "take-home" packets, which include a copy of the puppy's health certificate and records thus far, the puppy's pedigree and registration papers, copies of the parents' health clearances and the breeder's sales contract. Good breeders also supply literature on the breed and how to properly raise a Springer pup. A dedicated breeder knows that the more you know, the better life ahead will be for his precious Springer pup. Your goal must be to find one of those breeders.

FINDING THE RIGHT PUPPY

Overview

- Take your time, visit several litters and don't rush. The choice of your new four-legged family member is a major decision.
- The pups should have been raised among people so that their socialization began early on. This is very important to their development.
- You must meet the dam of the litter; the sire may not be on the premises, so you will at least want to see his pedigree and learn about him.
- Take the breeder's advice about the best pup for you, your lifestyle and your intentions. He also will have good information about caring for your new pup.

Welcoming the Puppy

Preparation for your pup's arrival begins well before you bring him home. For your puppy's personal safety (and to preserve your house and furnishings), you need to puppy-proof indoors and out before your pup comes home. You won't have time once he arrives! In addition to keeping him safe, puppy-proofing will allow you to enjoy, not worry about, your puppy, knowing that he is safe from common household dangers.

You should also stock up on the essential puppy supplies beforehand. Start with basic necessities and save the cute puppy goodies until later,

Your pup should meet all members of the family, two- and four-legged alike, and introductions should always be supervised. It didn't take these two long to snuggle up, but you have to keep a careful eye on interactions between your pets.

once the pup is past the chewing and wetting stage. Puppy stuff is often too cute to resist and can seriously dent your dog budget in the blink of an eye! First we will discuss some of the puppy necessities that you should have on hand:

Food and water bowls: You'll need two separate serving pieces, one for food and one for water. Stainless steel dog dishes are your best choice, as they are chew-proof and easy to clean. "Spaniel dishes," specifically designed to allow long ears to stay out of the dish, therefore keeping them clean, are a good investment for Springer owners.

Let your pup investigate his new backyard under your watchful eye. The yard should be securely fenced and truly escape-proof.

Puppy food: Your Springer puppy should be fed a quality food that is appropriate for his age and breed size. Your Springer puppy will start with medium-breed growth food, which should be his diet for his first year. While protein and fat content of a growth-formula food will be higher

Provide safe chew toys for your oral Springer pup. It's never too early to encourage proper chewing habits.

than that of an adult food, levels should not be too high to promote rapid growth. A good puppy food promotes healthy growth at a steady pace. For experienced recommendations, check with your breeder and your vet.

Collars and ID tag: Your Springer pup should have a collar that expands to fit him as he grows. Lightweight yet durable nylon adjustable collars work best for both pups and adult dogs. Put the collar on as soon as your pup comes home so he can get used to wearing it.

The ID tag should have your phone number, name and address, but not the puppy's name, as that would enable a stranger to identify and call your dog. Some owners include a line that says "Dog needs medication" to hopefully speed the dog's return if he is lost or stolen. Attach the tag with an "O" ring (the kind used in key rings), as the more common

"S" ring snags on carpets and comes off easily.

Leashes: A narrow six-foot leather or woven nylon leash is best for house-training, walks, puppy training classes and learning to walk properly on leash. Once he has polite leash manners, you may consider a retractable lead. This is an extendable lead that is housed in a large plastic handle; it extends or retracts with the push of a button. Retractable leads are available in several lengths (8 feet to 26 feet) and for different weight ranges, so buy one that will suit your Springer's adult size. These leads are especially handy for exercising your puppy in unfenced areas or when traveling with your dog.

Crating and gating: These will be your most important puppy purchases. A crate is the most valuable tool for housebreaking your pup, and your pup's favorite place to

Springers are great family pets. Bringing home your new puppy is a very special time, especially for children.

feel secure. Crates come in three varieties: wire, fabric mesh and the familiar plastic or fiberglass airline-type design. Wire or fabric-mesh crates offer the best ventilation, and some conveniently fold up suitcase-style. A fabric-mesh crate might, however, be a little risky for the youngster who likes to dig and chew.

Whatever your choice, purchase an adult-size crate, about 36 inches long by 24 inches wide by 28 inches high, rather than a small or puppy size; your Springer will soon grow into it. Crates often come with removable divider panels so you can create a smaller area for the pup and expand it as he grows. A too-large crate will not be useful for house-training, nor will it be a cozy den if the pup feels lost in it!

Well-placed baby gates will protect your house from the inevitable puppy mischief and thus save your sanity as well. Gated to a safe area near his potty exit, where he cannot wreak havoc or destruction, the puppy will soon master house-training, chew only appropriate chew toys rather than the legs of your antique chair and spare himself unnecessary corrections for the normal puppy mishaps that would happen if he were allowed to roam freely.

Gated, however, does not mean unsupervised. Springers bore easily and have been known to entertain themselves by chewing on doors and cabinetry. If your puppy must be unattended, use his crate.

Bedding: Dog beds are just plain fun, but don't go crazy just yet! Better to save that fancy bed for when your Springer is older and less likely to shred it up or make a puddle on it. For puppy bedding, it's best to use a few large towels, a mat or a blanket that can be laundered easily and often.

Grooming tools: Springers do require a certain amount of grooming. You will need a a slicker brush and a medium-tooth dog comb to maintain an adult's coat in clean and shiny condition, but a soft-bristled brush will suffice for the young puppy coat. Introduce your puppy to gentle grooming early on so he learns to like it.

Toys: Puppies, especially "birdy" breeds like the Springer, love all sorts of fuzzy toys that they can fetch and carry about. Eventually, though, most puppies shred their fuzzy stuffed toys, which is your cue to remove them!

Safe chew objects are a must if you hope to direct your Springer's chewing into acceptable habits. Sturdy nylon and rubber toys and hard sterilized bones come in age-appropriate sizes. All dogs love rawhides, but they can be dangerous if pieces are swallowed and thus should be offered only under super-vision.

Shoes, socks and slippers are off limits, since even a smart pup can't distinguish between your old loafers that you allow him to chew, from your new Italian leather boots that are strictly forbidden. Also avoid soft, squishy rubber toys or ones with button eyes that could be swallowed in a blink. Here's another important puppy-toy rule: offer only two or three toys at a time and rotate them to maintain pup's interest.

SOCIALIZATION

Puppy socialization is your Springer's insurance policy to a happy, stable adulthood and is, without question, the most important element in a

Puppy Safety at Home

After puppy shopping, you must puppy-proof your house. English Springer pups are naturally curious critters that will investigate everything new, then seek-and-destroy just because it's fun. The message here is: never let your puppy roam your house unsupervised. Scout your house for the following hazards:

Trash Cans and Diaper Pails
These are natural puppy magnets (they know where the good smelly stuff is!)

Medication Bottles, Cleaning Materials, Roach and Rodent Poisons
Lock these up. You'll be amazed at what a determined puppy can find.

Electrical Cords
Unplug wherever you can and make the others inaccessible. Injuries from chewed electrical cords are extremely common in young dogs.

Dental Floss, Yarn, Needles and Thread and Other Stringy Stuff
Puppies snuffling about at ground level will find and ingest the tiniest of objects and will end up in surgery. Most vets can tell you stories about the stuff they've surgically removed from puppies' guts.

Toilet Bowl Cleaners
If you have them, throw them out now. All dogs are born with "toilet sonar" and quickly discover that the water there is always cold.

Garage
Beware of antifreeze! It is extremely toxic and even a few drops will kill an adult Springer, less for a pup. Lock it and all other chemicals well out of reach. Fertilizers can also be toxic to dogs.

Socks and Underwear, Shoes and Slippers, Too
Keep them off the floor and close your closet doors. Puppies love all of the above because they smell like you times 10!

Springer puppy's introduction to the human world. Although Springers are by nature outgoing and gregarious dogs, it is still most important to expose them to strangers and new situations at an early age. Canine research has proven that unsocialized pups grow up to be spooky and insecure, and fearful of people, children and strange places. Many turn into fear biters or become

Ten-week-old Kahlua's body language is unmistakable: "I want to play!"

aggressive with other dogs, strangers and even family members. Puppy socialization lays the foundation for a well-behaved adult canine.

A canine's primary social-ization period occurs during the puppy's first 20 weeks of life. Once he leaves the safety of his mom and littermates at eight to ten weeks of age, your job begins. Start with a quiet, uncomplicated household for the first day or two, then gradually introduce him to the sights and sounds of his new human world. Frequent inter-action with new people and other dogs is essential at this age. As long as he's complete on his vaccinations, you can start to visit new places (dog-friendly, of course). Keep these new situations non-threat-ening, upbeat and positive. "Positive" is especially important when visiting your veterinarian. You don't want a pup that quakes with fear every time he sets a paw inside his doctor's office.

Your puppy also will need plenty of supervised exposure to children. Puppies of all breeds tend to view children as littermates and may attempt to exert the upper paw (a dominance ploy) over them. Because he was bred to hunt and carry game, a Springer pup may try to mouth a child's hands and fingers. Adult family members should supervise and teach the puppy not to bite or jump up on the kids, and teach the kids how to behave around the puppy.

Take your Springer youngster to puppy school. A good puppy class teaches proper canine social etiquette rather than rigid obedience skills. Your puppy will meet and play with young dogs of other breeds, and you will learn about the positive teaching tools you'll need to train your pup.

Remember this: there is a direct correlation between the quality and amount of time you spend with your puppy during his first 20 weeks of life and the character of the adult dog he will become. You cannot recapture this valuable learning period, so make the most of it.

WELCOMING THE PUPPY

Overview

- Prepare your home and have all of the necessary puppy supplies on hand in advance of your pup's arrival home.
- Puppy-proofing the home means creating a safe environment for your new arrival. Think of the many things in the home that can cause him harm and keep them well out of his reach.
- Supplies for your puppy include food, bowls, a collar and leash, ID tags, grooming equipment and, perhaps most importantly, a suitably sized crate with bedding.
- Socialization is a way of "puppy-proofing" your pup, helping his transition from canine to human pack and building his confidence in all types of situations.

House-training Your Springer

Most puppy owners dread the prospect of house-training their new puppy. Thoughts of piles and puddles on the carpet strike fear into their hearts. But there is an easier way…it's called the dog crate. Experienced dog owners and trainers emphasize that crates are the most logical and humane approach to house-training and that all pups will learn to love their crates if they are properly introduced. Because canines are natural den creatures, thanks to the thousands of years that their ancestors spent living in caves and cavities in the

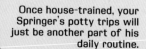

Once house-trained, your Springer's potty trips will just be another part of his daily routine.

ground, the crate appeals to their ancestral instincts. In short order, your puppy will consider his crate his personal home-within-a-home and adapt quite naturally to crate confinement. Your Springer puppy also is inherently clean and will prefer not to soil his "den" or living space, so the crate is a logical house-training aid.

If using papers to get you started, some recommend leaving down one soiled piece of paper so that the pup will sniff the area and know what to do.

So there you have it…a multi-purpose dog accessory, your Springer's personal den, a humane house-training tool, a way to keep puppy safe when unsupervised, a security measure that will protect your house and belongings when you're not home, a travel aid to house and protect your dog when you are traveling (most motels will accept a crated dog) and, finally, a comfy dog space for your puppy when your anti-dog relatives come to visit. What's not to love about the dog crate?

The basis of crate-training is that puppies do not want to soil their "dens" and thus will learn appropriate control when the crate is used properly.

Most experienced breeders insist on crate use after their puppies leave, and a few even crate-train their pups before they send them home. But it's more likely that your pup has never seen a crate, so it's up to you to make sure his introduction to the crate is a pleasant one. Introduce the crate as soon as he comes home so he learns that this is his new "house." This is best accomplished with dog treats. For the first day or two, toss a tiny treat into the crate each time you want him to go in. Pick a crate command, such as "Kennel," "Inside" or "Crate," and use it every time he enters. You also can feed his first few meals inside the crate with the door still open to make the crate association a happy one.

Your puppy should sleep in his crate from his very first night. He may whine at first and object to the confine-ment, but be strong and stay the course. If you release him when he cries, you provide his first life lesson…if I cry, I get out and maybe hugged. Your attention is a reward for his crying, so you'll see why that's not such a good plan after all.

A better scheme is to place the crate next to your bed at night for the first few weeks. Your presence will comfort him, and you'll also know if he needs a middle-of-the-night potty trip. Whatever you do, do not lend comfort by taking the puppy into bed with you. To a dog, on the bed means equal, which is not a good idea this early on as you are trying to establish yourself as puppy's leader.

Make a practice of placing your puppy in his crate for naps, at nighttime and whenever you are unable to watch him closely. Not to worry…he will let you know when he wakes up and needs a potty trip. If he falls asleep under the table or on the living-room carpet, guess what he'll do first when he wakes up? Make a puddle, and then toddle over to say "Hi!" He won't, however, be likely to soil his crate.

Become a Springer vigilante. Puppies always "go" when they wake up (quickly now!), within a few minutes after eating, after play periods and after brief periods of confinement. Also be aware of his water intake. Here's a house-training hint: try not to feed the puppy past 6:30 p.m. to aid in reducing nighttime potty trips.

Most pups under 12 weeks of age will need to eliminate at least every hour or so, or around 10 times a day (set your oven timer to remind you). Routines, consistency and an eagle eye are your keys to house-training success. Always take the puppy outside on his leash to the same area, telling him "Outside" as you go out. Pick a "potty" word ("Hurry up," "Go potty" and "Get busy" are some that are commonly used) and use it when he does his business, lavishing "Good puppy" praise on him and repeating your keyword.

Always use the same exit door for your potty trips and confine the puppy near the

A sturdy wire pen can be a good means of confining the pup to a particular area in the house, although a fully enclosed crate is best for when the pup is home alone or completely unsupervised.

exit area so he can find the door when he needs it. When he goes to the door, don't delay. Get his leash on and get him outside. Also watch for sniffing, circling or other signs that signal he has to relieve himself. Don't allow him to roam the house until he's house-trained...how will he find that outside door if he's three or four rooms away?

Of course, your puppy will have accidents. All puppies do. If you catch him in the act, clap your hands loudly, say "Aaah! Aaah!" and scoop him up to go outside. Your voice should startle him and make him stop (not to worry if he still drips a little as you carry him). Be sure to praise when he finishes his duty outside.

If you discover the piddle spot after the fact...more than three or four seconds later...you're too late. Pups only understand in the moment and will not understand a correction given

more than five (yes, that's only five) seconds after the deed. Correcting any later will only cause fear and confusion. Just forget it and vow to be more vigilant.

Never, and I mean *never*, rub your puppy's nose in his mistake or strike your puppy or adult dog with your hand, a newspaper or another object to correct him. He will not understand your "message" and will only become fearful of the person who is hitting him.

Despite its many benefits, crate use can be abused. Puppies under 12 weeks of age should never be confined for more than 2 hours at a time, unless, of course, they are sleeping. A general rule of thumb is three hours maximum for a three-month-old pup, four to five hours for the four- to five-month-old and no more than six hours for dogs over six months of age. If you're unable to be home to release the dog,

If paper-training, you will bring your pup to the papered area just as you would bring him to his chosen relief spot outdoors.

arrange for a relative, neighbor or dog-sitter to let him out to exercise and potty.

One final, but most important, rule of crate use: never, *ever*, use the crate for punishment. Successful crate use depends on your puppy's positive association with his "house." If the crate represents punishment or "bad dog stuff," he will resist using it as his safe place. Sure, you can crate your pup to keep him from getting underfoot as you clean up after he has sorted through the trash. Just don't do it in an angry fashion or tell him "Bad dog, crate!" Wait a few minutes, then happily place him in the crate with a treat while you clean up the mess.

Remember that successful house-training revolves around consistency and repetition. Maintain a strict schedule and use your keywords consistently. Well-trained owners have well-trained pups...and clean houses!

HOUSE-TRAINING YOUR SPRINGER

Overview

- When the crate is used correctly, crate-training is the most effective and humane house-training method.
- The success of crate-training has to do with the pup's viewing his crate as his personal den and not wanting to make a mess in it.
- Begin accustoming your pup to the crate on his very first day home, using treats to coax him into the crate for short periods of time. Crate time should always be happy time!
- Timing, consistency, frequency and praise are key elements in house-training success. Rewards and corrections will be effective only if you catch the pup in the act.
- As a pup gets older, he gains more control over his bodily functions and will not need potty trips as often.

Puppy Kindergarten

There are good reasons why the English Springer Spaniel is the hunting sweetheart of the spaniel breeds. As pups and adults, they brim with energy, always ready for action, games or training sessions. Bright and anxious to please, they are easily trained as long as the trainer does so with a gentle hand.

As with any breed of dog, the operative word here is "train." A Springer won't learn the house rules all by himself. A solid education in obedience, with you as the puppy's undisputed pack leader, is necessary

A puppy is a "blank slate" whose views of right and wrong behavior are shaped according to how you teach him.

to teach your Springer how to behave in his new human world. These lessons start on the day that you bring your puppy home.

All dogs are pack animals and, as such, they need a leader. Your Springer's first boss was his mother, and all of his early life lessons came from his mom and littermates. When he played too rough or nipped too hard, his siblings cried and stopped the game. When he got pushy or obnoxious, his mother cuffed him gently with a maternal paw. Now you have to assume that role of leader and communicate appropriate behavior in terms that his young canine mind will understand. Remember that he has no concept of our human rules; even if he did, from a canine perspective, those rules would make no sense at all!

When you start the teaching process, keep this thought uppermost: the first 20 weeks of any

A puppy must be amenable to handling, such as your examining his teeth and being able to remove items from his mouth.

Treats are helpful aids in training, both to gain your pup's attention and to teach him by rewarding for correct behavior.

canine's life are his most valuable learning time, a period when his mind is best able to soak up every lesson, both positive and negative. We've mentioned this already, but it's worth repeating! Positive experiences and

Toys can also be used as rewards. Learn what motivates your dog and dispense rewards accordingly; one thing you can never skimp on, though, is verbal praise.

proper socialization during this period are critical to your pup's future development and stability. An indisputable canine rule dictates that the amount and quality of time you invest with your Springer youngster now will determine what kind of an adult he will become. A wild dog, or a polite gentleman or lady? A well-behaved canine citizen

or a naughty mischief-maker? It's up to you.

Canine behavioral science tells us that any behavior that is rewarded will be repeated. That's called positive reinforcement. If something good happens, like a tasty treat or hugs and kisses, a puppy will naturally want to repeat the behavior. That same research also has proven that one of the best ways to a puppy's mind is through his stomach. Never underestimate the power of a treat! This leads to a very important puppy rule: keep your pockets full of small puppy treats at all times so that you are prepared to reinforce good behavior whenever it occurs.

That same reinforcement principle also applies to negative behavior, or what we humans might consider negative, like digging in the trash can, which the dog or puppy does not know is "wrong." If the pup gets into the garbage, steals food or does anything else that he thinks is fun or makes him feel good, he will do it again…it's a "self-rewarding" behavior. What better reason to keep a sharp eye on your puppy to prevent those normal canine behaviors? With a firm "No" and then a treat or hug when he stops the bad behavior, he will learn what *not* to do and that there are rewards for being good.

You are about to begin Puppy Class 101. Here are two simple rules to get you started. First, the puppy must learn that you are now the "alpha dog" and his new pack leader. Second, you have to teach him in a manner he will understand (sorry, barking just won't do it). Remember always that your pup knows nothing about human standards of behavior.

WORD ASSOCIATION

Use the same word (command) for each behavior every time you teach it, adding food rewards and verbal praise to reinforce the positive. The pup will make the connection and will be motivated to repeat the behavior when he hears those keywords. For example, when teaching the pup to potty outside, use the same potty term ("Go potty," "Get busy," "Hurry," etc.) each time he eliminates, adding a "Good boy!" while he's urinating. Your pup will soon learn what those trips outside are for.

TIMING

All dogs learn their lessons in the present tense. You have to catch them in the act (good or bad) in order to dispense rewards or discipline. You have three to five seconds to connect with him or he will not understand what he did wrong; thus, timing and consistency are your keys to success in teaching any new behavior or correcting bad behaviors. Remember also that the canine brain is not capable of premeditation. They do not "get even" or do something naughty "on purpose." Dogs live and learn in the present, reacting to whatever stimulus is present.

BASIC PRINCIPLES FOR SUCCESS

Successful puppy training depends on several important principles:

Basic exercises like the sit will be picked up quickly by a bright Springer puppy.

1. Use simple one-word commands and say them only once; otherwise, puppy learns that "Come" (or "Sit" or "Down") is a three- or four-word command. Even when a command is two words ("Go potty"), you say it as one word.

2. Never correct your dog for something he did minutes earlier. Three to five seconds, remember?

3. Always praise (and treat) as soon as he does something good (or when he stops doing something naughty). How else will your puppy know he's a good dog?

4. Be consistent. You can't snuggle together on the couch to watch TV today, then scold him for climbing on the couch tomorrow.

5. Never tell your dog to come to you and then correct him for something he did wrong. He will think the correction is for coming to you. (Think like a dog, remember?) Always go to the dog to stop unwanted behavior, but be sure that you catch him in the act or

your correction will not be understood.

6. Never hit or kick your dog or strike him with your hand, a newspaper or any object. Such physical measures will only create fear and confusion in your dog and could provoke aggressive behavior down the road.

7. When praising or correcting, use your best doggie voice. Use a light and happy voice for praise and a firm, sharp voice for warnings or corrections. A whiny "No, No" or "Drop that" will not sound too convincing, nor will a deep, gruff voice that says "Good boy" make your puppy feel like having fun. Your dog also will respond accordingly to family arguments. If there's a shouting match, he will think that he did something wrong and head for cover. So never argue in front of the kids *or* the dog!

PUPPY KINDERGARTEN

Overview

- Your puppy knows nothing of your house rules. Take advantage of your pup's aptitude for learning at this stage in his life, and be consistent in teaching him what is and is not acceptable behavior.
- Positive-reinforcement training is based on rewarding when a pup performs correctly or stops an undesirable behavior. Rewards include treats, toys, petting and, most importantly, verbal praise.
- When training, remember the basics: use simple commands, be careful with your timing and try to approach things from your pup's point of view.
- Acquaint yourself with the basic principles of training before you get started and, most importantly, implement them.

ENGLISH SPRINGER
SPANIEL

Basic Commands for Puppy

A little gentle pressure on the dog's rump will guide him into the sit position to show him what he should do when you say "Sit."

English Springer Spaniel puppies are bright little fellows who are eager to please and highly trainable. Your puppy will enjoy learning new things and will, in fact, look forward to his lessons. Keep the sessions short and happy and he'll soon become a canine good citizen of whom you will be proud. He will need to master basic commands such as come, sit, stay, down and heel, which are the foundation elements of good doggie manners and safety.

You can start your puppy's education as soon as he comes home. Don't worry, he's not too young. This is his prime learning period, so the earlier you start, the easier the process and the more successful you both will be. Always start your teaching exercises in a quiet, distraction-free environment; if outdoors, a fenced or otherwise enclosed area. Once your Springer pup has mastered any task, change the setting and practice in a different location like another room or the yard, and then progress to lessons with another person or a dog nearby. If the pup reacts to the new distraction and does not perform the exercise, back up and continue with the exercise but without the distractions for a while.

What a pleasure it is to walk a well-mannered Springer! You don't want your dog to take *you* for a walk.

Appoint one person to instruct your puppy in the early stages so as not to confuse the pup. It's the too-many-cooks rule of dog training. Once your smart Springer puppy has learned a

Your efforts in training will reward you with a dog who is well behaved in all situations.

command reliably, other family members can join in.

Ignore your Springer puppy for a few minutes before each training session. The lack of stimulation will make him more eager for your company and attention. Keep sessions short so your puppy won't get bored or lose his enthusiasm. In time he will be able to concentrate for longer periods. Vary the exercises to keep his enthusiasm level high. Watch for signs of boredom and loss of attention. Once you've lost his attention, it's better to stop the session and try again later.

Always keep your training sessions positive and upbeat. Use lots of praise, praise and more praise! Never train your puppy or adult dog if you are in a grumpy mood. You will lose patience and he will think that it is his fault, which will only reverse any progress that the two of you have made.

Finish every training session on a positive note. If you have been struggling or unsuccessful with an exercise, switch gears and do something he knows well (like "Sit") to end the session. This way, the puppy feels confident and training remains a positive experience for him.

ATTENTION AND NAME RECOGNITION

Before you can effectively teach your puppy any command, two things must happen. First, the puppy must learn to respond to his name (name recognition); second, you must be able to gain and hold his attention. How to accomplish that? Why, with treats, of course! Treats are defined as tiny tidbits, preferably pieces of something soft and easy to chew. We don't want to overfeed this pup. Thin slices of hot dogs cut in quarters work well.

Start by calling your Springer puppy's name. Once.

Not two or three times, but once. Otherwise he will learn he has a three-part name and will ignore you when you say it just once. Begin by using his name when he is undistracted and you are sure that he will look at you, and pop him a treat as soon as he does so. Repeat about a dozen times, several times a day. It won't take more than a day or so before he understands that his name means something good to eat.

ESTABLISH A RELEASE COMMAND

Your release command is the word you'll use to tell your pup that the exercise is over, similar to "At ease" in the military. "All done," "Free" and "Okay" are examples of commonly used release words. You'll need this release word so your Springer will know that the exercise is finished and it's okay for him to relax and/or move from a stationary position.

TAKE IT AND LEAVE IT

These commands offer too many advantages to list. Place a treat in the palm of your hand and tell your puppy to "Take it" as he grabs the treat. Repeat three times. On the

You want your Springer to look up at you, and thus up *to* you, with total attention on the task at hand.

fourth time, do not say a word as your dog reaches for the treat, just close your fingers around the treat and wait. Do not pull away, but be prepared for the pup to paw, lick, bark and nibble on your fingers. Patience! When he finally pulls away from your hand and waits for a few seconds, open your hand and tell him to "Take it."

Now for the next step. Show your Springer the treat in the palm of your hand and tell him to "Leave it." When he goes for the treat, close your hand and repeat "Leave it." Repeat the process until he pulls away, wait just a second, then open your hand and tell him to "Take it," allowing him to take the treat. Repeat the "Leave it" process until he waits just a few seconds, then give the treat on "Take it." Gradually extend the time you wait after your puppy "Leaves it" and before you tell him to "Take it."

Now you want to teach your Springer to leave things on the ground, not just in your hand (think of all the things that you don't want him to pick up). With your puppy on a loose leash, position yourself in front of him and toss a treat behind

you and a little to the side so he can see it, while saying "Leave it."

Here begins the dance. If he goes for the treat, use your body, not your hands, to block him, moving him backwards away from it. As soon as he backs off and gives up trying to get around you, unblock the treat and tell him to "Take it." Be ready to block again if he goes for it before you give permission. Repeat the process until he under-stands and waits for the command.

Once your Springer knows this well, practice with his food dish, telling him to "Leave it" and then "Take it" after he complies (he can either sit or stand while waiting for his dish). As before, gradually extend the waiting period before you tell him to "Take it." This little training exercise sends many messages to your Springer. He is reminded that you're the boss and that all good things, like food, come from the human who loves him. It will help prevent your puppy from becoming possessive of his food bowl, a behavior that only escalates and leads to more serious aggressive behaviors. The benefits of a solid take it/leave it are endless.

COME COMMAND

This command has life-saving potential. If your Springer were to run into the street, go after a squirrel, chase a child on a bike, break his leash or otherwise get away from you, you'd need to be able to call him back. This command is the most important for your Springer's safety.

Always practice the come command on leash and in a safely confined area. You can't afford to risk failure or the pup will learn that he does not have to come when called. Once you have the pup's attention, call him from a short distance: "Puppy, come!" (use your happy voice)

and give a treat when he comes to you. If he hesitates, tug him to you gently with his leash. Grasp and hold his collar with one hand as you dispense the treat. The collar grasp is important. You will eventually phase out the treat and switch to hands-on praise only. This maneuver also connects holding his collar with coming and treating, which will assist you in countless future behaviors.

Do 10 or 12 repetitions, 2 or 3 times a day. Once your pup has mastered the come on his leash, you can progress to using a long line, such as a lightweight rope that is 10 or 12 feet long. Continue to practice daily to imprint this most important behavior onto his tiny brain. You can progress to practicing off leash in your fenced yard only when he is reliably responding to the command on a long line.

Experienced Springer owners know, however, that

you can never completely trust a dog to come when called if the dog is bent on a self-appointed mission. Sporting dogs are bred to follow their noses, so off leash is often synonymous with out of control. Always keep your Springer on a leash when not in a fenced or confined area.

SIT COMMAND

This one's a snap, since your Springer already understands the treating process. Stand in front of your pup, move the treat directly over his nose and slowly move it backwards over his head. As he folds backwards to reach the goodie, his rear end will move downward to the floor. If the puppy raises up or stands to reach the treat, just lower it a bit. The moment his behind is down, tell him to "Sit." That's one word, "Sit." Release the treat and gently grasp the collar as you did with "Come." He will again make

that positive connection between the treat, the sit position and the collar hold.

As he becomes more proficient, make him hold the sit position longer before you give the treat (this is the beginning of the stay command). Begin using your release word to release him from the sit position. Practice using the sit command for everyday activities, such as sitting for his food bowl or a toy, and do random sits throughout the day. Make a game of the command, always for a food or praise "prize." Once he is reliable, combine the "Sit" and "Leave it" for his food dish. Your Springer is expanding his vocabulary.

STAY COMMAND

"Stay" is really just an extension of "Sit," which your Springer already knows. With the puppy sitting in front of you as commanded, place the palm of your hand in front of his nose and tell him to "Stay." Count to five. Give him his release word to end the stay and praise him. Stretch out the stays in tiny increments, making allowances for puppy energy.

Once he stays reliably, move your body a step backward after giving the command, then step up again. Gradually extend the time and distance that you move away. If the puppy moves, say "No" and move in front of him. Use sensible timelines, depending on your puppy's attention span.

DOWN COMMAND

Down can be a tough command to master. Because the down position is a submissive one, some dogs and certain take-charge breeds may find it especially difficult. That's why it's most important to teach this command to dogs when they are very young. The older they get, the more difficult it will be.

From the sit position, move the food lure from his nose to the ground and slightly backwards between his front paws. Wiggle the treat as necessary to attract the pup's attention. As soon as his front legs and rear end hit the floor, give the treat and tell him "Down, good boy, Down!" to connect the word

to the behavior. "Down" may prove difficult, so be patient and generous with the praise when he cooperates. Once he goes into the down position with ease, incorporate the stay as you did with the sit. By six months of age, your puppy should be able to do a 5-minute solid sit/stay, ditto for a down/stay.

Be gentle and reassuring when teaching the down command, never forcing your dog into this position, which he views as a submissive one.

CHAPTER 9

LEASH WALKING/HEEL COMMAND

The formal heel command comes a bit later in the learning curve. A young Springer should be taught simply to walk politely on a leash, at or near your side. That is best accomplished

Once your Springer is well versed in the basics and is around one year of age, you can progress to higher levels of training, such as for agility competition.

when your pup is very young and small, instead of 40 or more pounds pulling you down the street.

Start leash training soon after your pup comes home. Simply attach his leash to his buckle collar and let him drag it around for a little while every day. Play a puppy game

with the leash on. Make wearing his leash a happy moment in his day. If he chews the leash, distract him with a play activity. You also can spray the leash with a bitter-tasting chew-deterrent product to make it taste unpleasant and therefore undesirable to chew.

After a few days, gather up the leash in a distraction-free zone of the house or yard and take just a few steps together. With your puppy on your left side, hold a treat lure at his eye level to encourage the puppy to walk next to you. Pat your knee and use a happy voice. Use the phrase "Let's go!" as you move forward, holding the treat low to keep him near. Take a few steps, give the treat and praise him. Move forward just a few steps each time.

Keep these sessions short and happy (30 seconds is a lot in puppy time). Never scold him or nag him into walking faster or slower, just encourage him with happy talk. Walk straight ahead at first, adding wide turns once he gets the hang of it.

Progress to 90-degree turns, using a gentle leash tug on the turns, a happy verbal "Let's go!" and, of course, a treat. Walk in short 10- to 20-second bursts with a happy break (use your release word) and brief play (nothing wild or crazy, hugs will do nicely) in between. Keep total training time short and always quit with success, even if just a few short steps.

Learning to heel is a must for pet and show dogs alike. You want walking with your Springer to be pleasurable for both of you.

Formal heeling will come much later with advanced instruction in a basic obedience class.

BASIC COMMANDS FOR PUPPY

Overview

- Get started training your pup in his first few days at home. Start with no distractions, in brief lessons, accounting for a young pup's short attention span.
- Before you begin with formal commands, be sure that the pup knows his name, that you can capture his attention and that you have a release word to let him know that an exercise is over.
- "Take it" and "Leave it" are important commands to control what your dog may and may not put in his mouth.
- The basic exercises are come, sit, down, heel and stay. These commands are essential for a well-mannered dog but just as important for his safety.

ENGLISH SPRINGER
SPANIEL

Home Care for Your Springer

Regular mouth exams and toothbrushing are important parts of your Springer's routine care at home, as neglect can lead to serious internal health problems.

A sk any dog owner...his dog's life is too doggone short. But there are many things we as owners can do to maintain our dogs in the best possible health, maximize their life expectancies and help them live out their years in health and comfort. Dogs generally have annual physical exams and more frequent veterinary visits as they age, but in between those trips to the vet, we are our dogs' healthcare providers at home!

The average Springer lives about 12 to 13 years. The quality of those years depends on a conscientious

home healthcare program. Although genetics and the environment certainly can influence a dog's longevity, the fact remains that you are the backbone of your Springer's health-maintenance program. Like the proverbial apple a day, your daily focus on canine wellness will help "keep the veterinarian away."

Of all regimens included in this chapter, two are, without question, the most important: weight control and dental hygiene.

Springer puppies are curious and alert creatures, always on the go. Be aware of what your pup is sticking his snooping sniffer into!

WEIGHT CONTROL

Veterinarians tell us that over 50% of the dogs they see are grossly overweight and that such obesity will take two to three years off a dog's life, given the strain it puts on the animal's heart, lungs and joints. To determine if your Springer is at a proper weight, you should be able to feel your dog's ribs beneath a thin layer of muscle with very gentle pressure on his rib

Everyone agrees...a Springer with fresh breath is just irresistible!

cage. When viewing your dog from above, you should be able to see a definite waistline; from the side, he should have an obvious tuck-up in his abdomen.

ORAL HYGIENE

The American Veterinary Dental Society states that 80% of dogs show signs of oral disease as early as age three. Further studies prove that good oral hygiene can add three to five years to a dog's life. Need I say more? (Quick, look at your dog's teeth!)

Danger signs include yellow and brown build-up of tartar along the gumline, red, inflamed gums and persistent bad breath. If neglected, these conditions will allow bacteria to accumulate in your dog's mouth and enter your dog's bloodstream through those damaged gums, increasing the risk for disease in vital organs such as the heart, liver and kidneys. It's also known that periodontal disease is a major contributor to kidney disease, which is a common cause of death in older dogs and highly preventable.

Your vet should examine your Springer's teeth and gums during his annual checkups to make sure they are clean and healthy. He may recommend a professional veterinary cleaning if there is excessive plaque build-up. During the other 364 days a year, brush the dog's teeth daily, or at least twice a week. Use a doggie toothbrush and use canine toothpaste flavored with chicken, beef or liver (minty people paste is harmful to dogs). If your dog resists a toothbrush, try a nappy washcloth or gauze pad wrapped around your finger. Start the brushing process with gentle gum massages when your Springer is very young so he will learn to tolerate and even enjoy getting his teeth cleaned.

Feeding dry dog food is an excellent way to help minimize plaque accumulation. You can also treat your dog to a raw carrot every day. Like dry dog food, carrots help scrub away plaque while providing extra vitamins A and C, and will not cause your dog to gain weight.

Invest in healthy chew objects, such as nylon or rubber bones and toys with ridges that act as tartar scrapers. These special dental chews are designed to remove and prevent plaque. Raw beef knuckle bones (cooked bones will splinter) also work, but watch for sharp edges and splintering on any chew object, which can cut the dog's mouth and also intestinal lining if swallowed. Rawhides do not digest easily and can cause choking if the dog swallows large chunks, as many dogs tend to do. If you offer rawhides, do so infrequently and only under supervision.

ROUTINE CHECKS

Your weekly grooming sessions should include body checks for lumps (cysts, warts and fatty tumors), hot spots and other skin or coat problems. While harmless

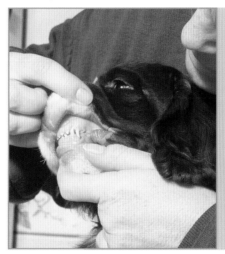

Start oral exams and gentle toothcare in puppyhood, when you will have a much easier time introducing your Springer to these procedures.

skin lumps are common in older dogs, many can be malignant, and your vet should examine any abnormality. Black mole-like patches or growths on any body part require immediate veterinary inspection. Remember, petting and hugging also can turn up little abnormalities.

Be extra-conscious of dry skin, a flaky coat and thinning hair, all signs of possible thyroid disease. Check for fleas and flea dirt (especially on your dog's underside and around the base of the tail) if you think fleas could be present.

EYE CARE

Your Springer's vision may deteriorate with age. A bluish haze is common in geriatric

Pay attention to your Springer's eyes and the areas around them for cleanliness and overall health.

dogs and does not impair vision, but you should always check with your vet about any changes in the eyes to determine if they are harmless or indicative of a problem.

THE OTHER END

How about his rear end? Does he chew at his rear or scoot and rub it on the carpet? That's a sign of impacted anal glands. Have your vet express those glands (it's not a job for amateurs). Have annual stool cultures done to check for intestinal parasites. Hook-, whip- and roundworms can cause weight and appetite loss, poor coat quality and all manner of intestinal problems as well as weaken your dog's resistance to other canine diseases. See your vet if any of those signs appear.

Tapeworms, common parasites that come from fleas, look like grains of rice tucked in the stool. If your dog's stool sample checks out as parasite-free, your vet may recommend a preventive. Usually this is a heartworm preventive that also protects against many of the other common internal parasites. It's up to you to remember to administer his preventives on schedule; many come in a once-monthly dose.

KNOW YOUR DOG!
Cultivate a keen awareness of even subtle changes in your dog. Research canine healthcare and first aid and add a detailed book on the topic to your library. Keep a list of symptoms, remedies and first-aid tips in a handy place to reference when necessary, along with your vet's and emergency vet's numbers. Your Springer's life could depend on it. For example, heart and kidney disease can occur in any dog, but both are very treatable if detected early. Your attention to his health maintenance and early detection of problems are the keys to your dog's longevity and quality of life.

HOME CARE FOR YOUR SPRINGER

Overview

- You are responsible for your dog's healthcare in between visits to the veterinarian.
- One of the most important home-care regimens is weight control. Obesity increases a dog's risk of health problems and diminishes his overall quality of life.
- Dental care is often overlooked but is highly important. Mouth disease is a major cause of internal problems and can effectively shorten a dog's life.
- Routine care for your Springer at home includes checking for evidence of external and internal parasites, being consistent with routine preventives, being aware of possible anal-sac problems and looking out for the health of his eyes.
- Know your dog! Noticing when he's not acting like his usual self is one of the best ways to recognize when something is wrong.

CHAPTER 11

Feeding Your Springer Spaniel

A proper diet is as important for healthy dogs as it is for healthy people. Your Springer needs to eat a quality food that is appropriate for his age and lifestyle. Only the premium (and usually higher-end) dog foods provide the proper balance of the vitamins, minerals and supplements that are necessary to support healthy bone, muscle, skin and coat.

The major dog-food manufacturers have done extensive research on canine nutrition and developed their

The easiest way to start feeding your pup is to continue with the same quality food that he was getting from the breeder.

formulas with strict controls, using only quality ingredients obtained from reliable sources. The labels on the food packaging detail the products in the food (beef, chicken, corn, etc), and they list ingredients in descending order of weight or amount in the food.

Some Springer puppies really get into their meals!

Don't be intimidated by all those dog-food bags on the store shelves. Read the labels on the bags (how else can you learn what's in those foods?) and call the information number on the dog-food bag with any questions you may have. A solid education in the basics of canine nutrition will provide the tools you need to offer your dog a diet that is best for his long-term health.

In the world of quality dog foods, there are enough choices to confuse even experienced dog folks. Today there are specific formulas designed for every breed size, age and activity level. Just as the diet of a human

Stainless steel bowls are good for orally-oriented pups like Springers, as these types of bowls are more resistant to chewing than plastic.

CHAPTER 11

infant differs from that of a human adult, puppies require a diet different from that of an adult canine. Puppy growth formulas contain protein and fat levels that are appropriate for different-sized dogs. Medium-sized dogs like your Springer require appropriate amounts of protein and fat during these early months of rapid growth, which is better for healthy joint development.

A good puppy food works with the puppy's natural growth rate and does not encourage him to grow too quickly, which can lead to skeletal disorders. Do not add your own vitamin supplements or table scraps to a nutritionally complete food. You will only upset the balance of the food, which could negatively affect the growth pattern of your Springer pup. Further, some "people foods," among them chocolate, nuts, raisins, grapes and onions, are toxic to dogs.

WHEN AND HOW TO FEED

Ask your breeder and your vet what food they recommend for your Springer pup. If you plan to switch from the food fed by your breeder, take home a small supply of the breeder's food to mix with your own to aid your puppy's adjustment to his new food.

An eight-week-old puppy does best eating three times a day. (Tiny tummy, tiny meals.) At about 16 weeks of age, you can switch to twice-daily feeding. Most breeders suggest two meals a day for the life of the dog, regardless of breed, as this is much healthier for a dog's digestion than one large daily portion. A Springer will do well on puppy food for his first year of life, after which he can be switched to an adult-maintenance food.

Free feeding, that is, leaving a bowl of food available all day, is not recommended. Free feeding fosters picky eating habits...a bite here, a nibble there. Free feeders are also more likely to become possessive of their food bowls, a problem behavior that signals the beginning of aggression.

Plan your Springer's meals at times when he will have adequate rest before and after eating. This is a good preventive against bloat, a deadly condition that can occur in most any dog—ask your vet about this and other precautions. Scheduled meals give you one more opportunity to remind your Springer that all good things in life come from you, his chef and leader! With scheduled meals, it's also easier to predict elimination, which is the better road to house-training. Regular meals help you know just how much your puppy eats and when, which is valuable information for weight control or if your dog's appetite changes, which could signal illness.

Allow your dog about 20 minutes to eat his food. Some will eat the whole bowl of food with gusto, while others may take their time and leisurely nibble at the food. Remove any food that remains after 20 minutes and do not add it to the next meal. If, at any time in your Springer's life, you feel that

The breeder starts the litter out on dry food as part of the weaning process.

he is becoming too picky, discuss that problem with your vet.

DRY OR CANNED FOOD?
Should you feed canned or dry food? Should you offer dry food with or without water? Dry food is recommended by most vets, since the dry particles help to

clean the dog's teeth of plaque and tartar. You should *always* add some water to your Springer's dry food. Feeding only dry food may contribute to your dog developing bloat—a potentially life-threatening condition. A bit of water added immediately

Puppies should be taught to behave politely while waiting for their bowls to be put down, meaning no begging or jumping up.

before eating is also thought to enhance the flavor of the food, while still preserving the dental benefits. Always have water available for your dog to drink at all times.

HOW MUCH FOOD?

Like people, puppies and adult dogs have different appetites; some will lick their food bowls clean and beg for more, while others pick at their food and leave some of it untouched. It's easy to overfeed a chow hound. Who can resist those soulful Springer eyes? Be strong and stay the right course. Chubby puppies may be cute and cuddly, but the extra weight will stress their growing joints and is thought to be a factor in the development of hip and elbow problems. Overweight pups also tend to grow into overweight adults who tire easily and will be more susceptible to other health problems. Seek advice from your breeder and vet about how to adjust meal portions as your puppy grows.

LEAN IS IN!

Always remember that lean is healthy and fat is not.

Research has proven that obesity is a major canine killer. Quite simply, a lean dog lives longer than one who is overweight, and that doesn't even reflect the better quality of life for the lean dog that can run, jump and play without the burden of an extra 10 or 20 pounds.

If your adult dog is overweight, you can switch to a "light" food that has fewer calories and more fiber. "Senior" foods for older dogs are formulated to meet the needs of less active, older dogs. "Performance" diets contain more fat and protein for dogs that compete in sporting disciplines or lead very active lives.

YOU ARE WHAT YOU EAT!

The bottom line is this: what and how much you feed your dog is a major factor in his overall health and longevity. It's worth your investment in extra time and dollars to provide the best diet for your dog.

FEEDING YOUR SPRINGER SPANIEL

Overview

- Manufactured dog foods come in many different formulas appropriate for different life stages and sizes of dog.
- Avoid supplementing or giving table scraps. These things can upset the balance of a dog's diet, cause stomach upset or weight gain or, even worse, be toxic to the dog.
- Scheduled mealtimes are the best way to feed a dog. The schedule will change as the pup matures, but the consistency is what is important for many reasons.
- As you learn your dog's eating habits, and with the guidelines on the food package, you will determine how much food your Springer needs daily to stay in good condition.

CHAPTER 12

ENGLISH SPRINGER
SPANIEL

Grooming
Your Springer

Regular brushing is the only way to keep your Springer's coat free of mats and tangles. It also will help control the excess dog hair that plagues most owners of double-coated breeds such as the Springer. Good grooming habits, established early in your Springer's life, are essential to his physical well-being. He should be brushed at least once a week. Coat care means checking for lumps, bumps, hot spots and other abnormalities that can hide beneath your dog's fur, or any tiny critters like fleas and ticks which may have crept aboard your dog.

Before your puppy leaves the breeder, he should have been introduced to a basic grooming routine. Grooming is not just for show dogs, but is important for the life-long health of your Springer.

Every dog should enjoy the hands-on grooming process. To that end, introduce the brush, nail clippers and toothbrush when he is just a pup. Dogs who have not experienced these ministrations early in life may object when they are older…and bigger…and better able to resist. Grooming will then become a distasteful chore, rather than a routine that both of you can enjoy.

Start grooming your puppy in short sessions, always keeping this time positive and enjoyable.

Hold your first grooming session as soon as your Springer puppy has adjusted to his new home base. Start with tiny increments of time, stroking him gently with a soft brush, briefly handling his paws, looking inside his ears and gently touching his gums. Use lots of encouraging sweet talk and offer little bits of dog treats. Ah, the power of positive association!

The adult Springer has a medium-length double coat, with an undercoat that varies in density depending on the climate in which he is raised.

Have a heavy towel on hand for drying your Springer's coat. Keep him away from drafts until he is completely dry.

Regular brushing will remove dust and distribute the oils that will keep his coat clean and conditioned. A Springer tends to shed lightly all year round, but if you notice times when he is shedding more heavily, more frequent brushing will help control the shed hair. Groom all the way down to the skin so that you are brushing through both layers of the coat.

Frequent bathing is seldom necessary and, in fact, will remove the essential oils that keep your dog's skin supple and his coat soft and gleaming. Bathe him with a good conditioning shampoo every couple of months, more often if he plays in mud holes or rolls around in something smelly (a favorite outdoor pastime).

Use a shampoo made for dogs, working it into a good lather and then rinsing thoroughly. Always be sure to rinse the coat completely to avoid any itching from residual shampoo. A good chamois is the ideal tool for drying, as it absorbs water like a sponge. Keep him away from drafts for a good while after bathing and drying to prevent chilling.

Nails should be trimmed about once a month. Offer puppy treats with each clipping lesson. At first you may have to settle on only one or two nails at a time; that's a good start. It is also better to trim a small amount of nail more frequently than trying to cut back a nail that has grown too long. Nip off the nail tip or clip at the curved part of the nail. Be careful not to cut the quick (the pink vein in the nail), as that is quite painful and the nail may bleed profusely. If you happen to snip a quick, you can stanch the bleeding with a few drops of a clotting solution available from your pet-supply store.

Weekly ear checks are worth the proverbial pound of

cure; you can incorporate this into your weekly brushing time. The Springer's ear flaps act like a terrarium cover that prevents air flow and keeps the ear canal moist and ripe for musty growths, especially in humid climates. Regular cleansing, especially after swimming, with a specially formulated ear cleanser obtained through your veterinarian will keep your dog's ears clean and odor-free. Use a cotton ball to clean the ear flap and the folds of the inner ear, but do not probe into the canal to avoid injuring the eardrum.

Symptoms of ear infection include redness and/or swelling of the ear flap or inner ear, a nasty odor and/or dark, waxy discharge. If your Springer digs at his ear(s) with his paw, shakes his head a lot or appears to lose his balance, see your vet at once. Be proactive with your Springer's ear care.

GROOMING YOUR SPRINGER

Overview

- Introduce your Springer to all of the routine grooming tasks when he is a puppy.
- Regular brushing keeps your Springer's coat free of painful mats and tangles, as well as distributes the skin's natural oils for a healthy shine.
- Too-frequent bathing is not recommended, as it will dry the skin and coat and alter the coat's natural water-repellent properties.
- Trim your dog's nails regularly. It's better to clip them frequently, a little at a time, than to let them grow too long and risk cutting into the quick.
- The Springer's drop ears create a warm environment in which bacteria can grow and infections sprout up. Pay attention to the condition and cleanliness of your dog's ears.

ENGLISH SPRINGER SPANIEL

Keeping Your Springer Active

For centuries, ancestors of the English Springer Spaniel served as splendid hunting companions for both kings and commoners. Today the Springer is still a favorite among sportsmen who enjoy hunting with a flushing breed. Though many modern Springers may never see a brace of pheasants, they still possess the same energy and pizzazz as their forebears and will need vigorous exercise and activities. The benefits extend beyond your Springer's

Over the field and through the woods...pure joy for a Springer in full flight.

health, since a well-exercised dog is happily tired and less inclined to find mischievous outlets for his unexpended energy.

That said, bear in mind that neither the Springer puppy nor adult will get proper exercise on his own. He needs a reason or incentive to keep moving and that incentive is, of necessity, the person in charge of his life. Two brisk daily walks will help keep your Springer fit and trim and keep his mind stimulated as he investigates the sights and sounds of the neighborhood.

The teeter-totter is one of the obstacles that dogs learn to navigate in agility training.

How long and how far to walk depends on your Springer's age, physical condition and energy level. When and where to walk is as important as how long. On warm days, avoid walking during midday heat and go out during the cooler morning or evening hours. If you're a jogger, your Springer buddy is the perfect running partner if he is in

Amid the frantic pace of the agility course, the dog is expected to stop on the pause table and assume the down position for a prescribed amount of time before continuing on with the obstacles.

good physical condition. Jogging on turf or another soft surface is easier on your Springer's joints and feet. Just make sure that your dog is healthy and fully developed before you invite him to join you on your mile-plus run.

A young Springer's bones are softer and more vulnerable to injury during his first year of life and should not be subjected to heavy stress. That means no games or activities that encourage high jumping or heavy impact on his front or rear until he is past the risky age. Playtime with other puppies and older dogs also should be supervised to avoid injury. Swimming in a safe area, whenever possible, is excellent exercise, as it puts no stress on the pup's growing frame. It also is excellent exercise for adults. Introduce your pup to water slowly and always supervise any swimming time.

Daily exercise times are also excellent bonding sessions for you and your dog. Your Springer will look forward eagerly to his special time with you. As a creature of habit, your dog will bounce with joy when he sees you don your cap, pick up his leash or rattle your house keys.

CLASSES AND COMPETITION
Consider taking your exercise program to another level. Plan a weekly night out with your Springer and enroll in a class. Obedience, maybe agility...or both! The benefits of obedience class are endless. You will be motivated to work with your dog daily at home so you don't look unprepared or unraveled at each week's class. You'll both be more active and thus healthier. Your dog will learn the basics of obedience, will be better behaved and will become a model citizen. He will

discover that you really are the boss...the goal of every dog owner!

Agility classes offer even more healthy outlets for Springer energy. He will learn to scale an A-frame ramp, race headlong through a tunnel, balance himself on a teeter-totter, jump up and off a platform, jump through a hoop, zig-zag between a line of posts and more. Agility training should not begin until the dog is 12 months of age to limit impact on those growing bones and muscles. The challenge of learning to navigate these agility obstacles, and his success in mastering each one with you by his side, will make you proud of both of you!

You can take both of these activities one step further and show your dog in obedience and agility competition. Shows and trials are held year-round and are designed for all levels of experience. Find a club or join a training group. Working with other fanciers will give you the incentive to keep working with your dog. Check the ESSFTA's and the AKC's websites for details and contact people to help you get started.

"Spirit," an American and Canadian Champion, an accomplished hunting, tracking, obedience and agility dog, was bred and is co-owned by the author. She "springs" through the tire jump with ease.

FIELD TRIALS AND HUNTING EVENTS

What better way to exercise and enjoy your Springer than doing what most Springers love best...flushing and retrieving birds? A Springer's love of bird work can range from mild to wildly passionate, depending on his working ancestry, but almost every Springer will enjoy time spent working in the field.

Both the AKC and the United Kennel Club, another large national dog organization, sponsor hunt tests, which are designed for the non-competitive sportsman who may or may not actually hunt. Field trials are for the true competitor, and if that is

Another type of jump on the agility course is the bar jump. The Springer's natural exuberance and trainability give him the potential for high achievements in agility.

your bent, make sure you have a pup with outstanding credentials before you consider entering the field-trial world. Pedigree is the name of this game. Your local breed or hunting club can refer you to groups who train specifically for such events. Rules and regulations for spaniel hunt tests are available on the AKC's (www.akc.org) and UKC's (www.ukcdogs.com) websites.

CONFORMATION

Conformation is by far the most popular canine competition activity for all breeds. If you plan to show your Springer, make sure you look for a show-quality puppy and discuss your goals with the breeder. Most local breed and kennel clubs host conformation training classes and can help novices get started with their pups. It's best to start learning show procedure and practicing when your Springer is young so he develops a good "ring" attitude.

WORKING CERTIFICATE TESTS

In 1960, the breed's parent club, the English Springer Spaniel Field Trial Association, launched the Working Certificate program to encourage breeders and exhibitors to keep the hunting instincts alive in the breed. Over time, the requirements were changed to make the tests available to a wider audience, with the latest update occurring in 1998.

The intent was stated: "To continue as basic tests of instincts and usefulness in the field; encourage owners to train their English Springer Spaniels to a hunting companion level; and serve as a first step towards involving new participants in AKC Hunting Tests for Spaniels."

The dogs are tested individually on land and in water, working beside their handlers in a manner consistent with actual upland hunting. The judges grade the dogs' performances as Excellent, which earns the WDX (Working Dog Excellent); Satisfactory, which earns the WD (Working Dog); or Poor, which is a failing score.

Training for field activities is as fun and rewarding for the handler as it is for the dog. Further information on working tests is available through the ESSFTA (www.essfta.org).

KEEPING YOUR SPRINGER ACTIVE

Overview

- Both show- and field-type Springers are high-energy dogs who love outdoor exercise and need such activity to keep fit and mentally stimulated.
- Walking your dog is good exercise for both of you and good bonding time, too. Take it easy for your Springer's first year, though.
- Obedience and agility are enjoyed by Springers and their owners whether just training or participating on a competitive level. Conformation showing is also popular for those with show-quality Springers.
- Field events are held on different levels so that working and non-working Springers alike can test their natural instincts. Events are organized and awards given by the AKC and the ESSFTA.

CHAPTER 14

ENGLISH SPRINGER SPANIEL

Your Springer and His Vet

As with other pre-puppy chores, it's important to connect with a good veterinarian before you bring your puppy home. The vet will be his primary healthcare provider, so check with your breeder, your dog-owning friends or your local kennel club for references. A good vet will plan your puppy's long-term healthcare and help you become dog-smart about canine health.

Take your puppy to your veterinarian within three or four days after you bring him home. Show the

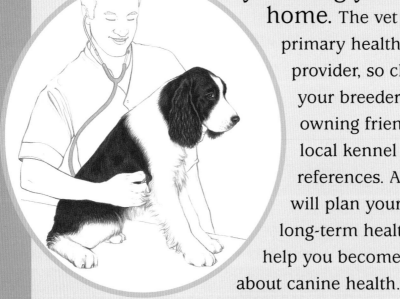

You and your dog both should have a good rapport with the vet, as he will be your dog's other lifetime best friend.

vet any health records of shots and wormings from your breeder. He will conduct a thorough physical exam to make sure your Springer pup is in good health and will work out a schedule for vaccinations and other routine visits. A good vet will be gentle with a new pup and do everything possible to make sure the puppy is not frightened or intimidated.

In addition to seeing that your Springer gets proper veterinary care, you also must be prepared for first-aid situations at home.

VACCINES

Vaccine protocol varies, but most vets recommend a series of three "combination" shots given at three- to four-week intervals. Your puppy should have had his first shot before he left his breeder. The wisest and most conservative course is to administer only one shot per visit, rather than a combination shot, and allow three weeks between shots, but combination shots are what are usually given.

A good vet will be gentle with your puppy so that even his shots will seem painless.

The vaccines recommended by the American Veterinary Medical Association (AVMA) are those which protect against diseases most dangerous to your puppy and adult dog. Called core vaccines, they include distemper, fatal in puppies; canine parvovirus, highly contagious and also fatal in puppies and at-risk dogs; canine adenovirus (CAV-2), highly contagious and high risk for pups under 16 weeks of age; and canine hepatitis (CAV-1), highly contagious, pups at high risk. These are generally given together in a combination shot. Rabies immunization is required in all 50 states, with the rabies vaccine given at least three weeks after the complete series of three puppy shots.

Vaccines no longer routinely recommended by the AVMA, except when the risk is present, are canine parainfluenza, leptospirosis, canine coronavirus, *Bordetella* (kennel cough) and Lyme disease (borreliosis). Your veterinarian should advise you if your Springer should be immunized against these diseases, based on the risk in your area and if you plan to travel with your dog.

CHECK-UPS
Every Springer should visit his veterinarian at least once a year. At the very least, he needs an annual heartworm test before he can receive another year of heartworm preventive medication. Most importantly, the annual visit keeps your vet apprised of your pet's health progress, and the hands-on exam often turns up small abnormalities that you can't see or feel.

As your Springer reaches his senior years, around eight years old or as the vet recommends it, he should start to visit the vet twice annually. Older dogs are more prone to health problems and more frequent visits allow the vet more chances to catch and treat problems early on.

HEARTWORM

This is a parasite that propagates inside your dog's heart and will ultimately kill your dog. Now found in all 50 states, heartworm is acquired through a mosquito bite. Heartworm preventive is a prescription medication available only through your veterinarian. A heartworm test is required before the vet will dispense the medication, which usually protects against other common internal parasites as well.

FLEAS AND TICKS

Fortunately, there are quite a few low-toxic effective preventives to aid you and your dog in your war against fleas and ticks. Three tick-borne diseases, Lyme disease (canine borreliosis), ehrlich-iosis and Rocky Mountain spotted fever, are now found in almost every state and can affect humans as well as dogs.

Imidacloprid is a spot-on treatment applied between the shoulder blades that will kill adult fleas for 30 days. Lufenuron is an insect growth regulator, given as a monthly pill, that prevents flea eggs from hatching. Fipronil is a spot-on treatment that will

Administering medication to a puppy can be quite a challenge! Liquid medicine is often given in a syringe-like dropper and squirted into the mouth...easier said than done!

kill fleas for 90 days and ticks for up to 30 days. Selamectin is a monthly spot-on that protects against heartworm, fleas, certain types of ticks and certain mites.

SPAY/NEUTER

Females spayed before their first heat cycle (estrus) have a

90% lower risk of several common female cancers and other serious problems. Males neutered before their male hormones kick in, usually before six months of age, enjoy greatly reduced to zero risk of testicular and prostate cancer and related problems. Additionally, neutered males will be less likely to roam, become aggressive or display certain overt male behaviors.

Having your Springer sexually altered will *not* automatically make him or her fat and lazy. Statistically, having your pet spayed or neutered will make a positive contribution to the pet overpopulation problem and, very importantly, to your dog's long-term health.

YOUR SPRINGER AND HIS VET

Overview

- Research vets in your area and have your vet chosen before puppy comes home, as one of the first things you will do with your pup is take him for an exam and possibly shots.
- Your vet will manage your Springer's vaccination program as well as the booster-shot schedule throughout the dog's life.
- Adult Springers need at least an annual physical exam, and vets usually recommend that senior dogs visit more frequently, twice yearly at the minimum.
- Dogs can fall prey to both internal and external parasites; your vet will check for these at your dog's exams and prescribe appropriate preventives.
- Spaying females and neutering males offer important health benefits to both sexes. Breeders should always require that pet-quality dogs be sexually altered at the recommended age.